THE HOPI

by Suzanne Freedman

Illustrated by Richard Smolinski

ROURKE PUBLICATIONS, INC.

VERO BEACH, FLORIDA 32964

CONTENTS

Library of Congress Cataloging-in-Publication Data

Freedman, Suzanne
    The Hopi / by Suzanne Freedman.
        p.   cm. — (Native American people)
    Includes index.
    Summary: Surveys various aspects of Hopi culture, including family life and daily activities, hunting and food gathering, clothing, games, religion, and social organization.
    ISBN 0-86625-601-6
    1. Hopi Indians—History—Juvenile literature. 2. Hopi Indians—Social life and customs—Juvenile literature. [1. Hopi Indians. 2. Indians of North America—Arizona.] I. Title. II. Series.
E99.H7F74 1997
973'.049745—dc21   96-53640
                                                    CIP
                                                    AC

Introduction

For many years archaeologists—and other people who study early Native American cultures—believed that the first humans to live in the Americas arrived in Alaska from Siberia between 11,000 and 12,000 years ago. Stone spear points and other artifacts dating to that time were discovered in many parts of the Americas.

The first Americans probably arrived by way of a vast bridge of land between Siberia and Alaska. The land link emerged from the sea when Ice Age glaciers lowered the level of the world's oceans.

The first migration across the bridge was most likely an accident. It appears that bands of hunters from Asia followed herds of mammoths, giant bison, and other Ice Age game that roamed the 1,000-mile-wide bridge. Over a long time—perhaps thousands of years—some of the hunters arrived in Alaska.

Many scholars now suggest that the first Americans may have arrived in North America as early as 30,000 or even 50,000 years ago. Some of these early Americans may not have crossed the bridge to the New World. They may have arrived by boat, working their way down the west coasts of North America and South America.

3

In support of this theory, scientists who study language or genetics (the study of the inherited similarities and differences found in living things) believe that there may have been many migrations of peoples over the bridge to North America. There are about 200 different Native American languages, which vary greatly. In addition to speaking different languages, groups of Native Americans can look as physically different as, for example, Italians and Swedes. These facts lead some scientists to suspect that multiple migrations started in different parts of Asia. If this is true, then Native Americans descend not from one people, but from many.

After they arrived in Alaska, different groups of early Americans fanned out over North and South America. They inhabited almost every corner of these two continents, from the shores of the Arctic Ocean, in the north, to Tierra del Fuego, at the southern tip of South America. Over this immense area, there were many different environments, which changed with the passage of time. The lifestyles of early Americans adapted to these environments and changed with them.

In what is now Mexico, some Native Americans built great cities and developed agriculture. Farming spread north. So did the concentration of people in large communities, which was the result of successful farming. In other regions of the Americas, agriculture was not as important. Wild animals and plants were the main sources of food for native hunters and gatherers. The Hopi were farmers. To supplement the food they grew, they gathered wild plants, and also fished and hunted.

Origins of the Hopi

The word *Hopi* means "peaceful." The tribe has farmed the desert land of northeastern Arizona for centuries, enduring many hardships, such as drought, crop failure, and disease epidemics. Anthropologists know a lot about the early history of the Hopi because their culture is one of the best preserved Native American cultures in North America.

No one knows exactly when the Hopi separated from other Southwest peoples. Nearly 2,000 years ago, the tribe's ancestors lived in the San Juan River Valley in what are now the states of Colorado, New Mexico, and Utah. These semi-nomadic people inhabited the broad territories on each side of the valley. They harvested wild food and cultivated maize (Indian corn), wandering back and forth across their large territory.

By A.D. 300, a group of people with a loosely knit culture established themselves in the region. They were the Anasazi. Immigrating groups brought knowledge of pottery making. Stone houses began to appear. By the eighth or ninth century, the natives were living in large apartments made of stone slabs or blocks. These apartments housed thousands of people. By the twelfth century, Native Americans in the San Juan River Valley were growing cotton for clothing and many varieties of maize for food.

It was probably a long drought toward the end of the thirteenth century that encouraged the tribes in this region to move south of the San Juan Valley. One course of migration was into the Rio Grande Valley in what is today New Mexico. The settlements along that river were later given the name pueblos by the Spanish. *Pueblo* means "town" or "townspeople."

Some family groups eventually moved toward the southern fringe of the Black Mesa region in the center of what is now Arizona. (A mesa looks like a small, isolated mountain with a flat top.) It was a dry country with no river and very little rainfall, and it gave no promise of large crops or easy work. One settlement after another rose at the edge of Black Mesa. The people who stayed in Black Mesa country were the Hopi.

The Hopi villages now standing are grouped along three extensions of Black Mesa: First (eastern) Mesa, Second (middle) Mesa, and Third (western) Mesa. The villages seem to be a part of the mesas themselves because the color and shape of Hopi homes resemble the landscape. For many miles in every direction are the sites of old villages that the Hopi claim belonged to their ancestors.

Even though much of this great stretch of country is now occupied by the Navajo tribe and by whites, the Hopi consider it to be their own special territory.

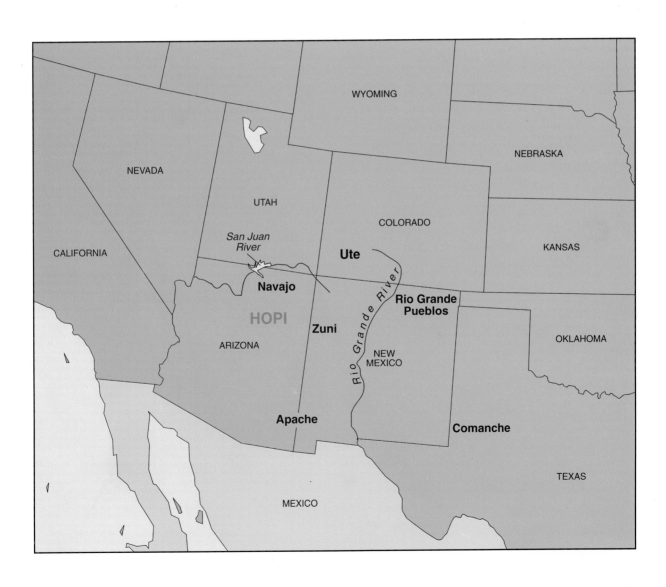

Daily Life

At sunrise, a Hopi village crier called people to begin their daily chores. Men cultivated small fields of corn, beans, squash, and melons. Women prepared the meals, cared for children, and did other household chores. Prayers began early in the day.

In the center of each of the Hopi's walled communities was a central village square, or plaza. In the plaza were the *kivas* where the men gathered. The *kivas* were underground, circular rooms, usually made of stone, with ladders or steps leading down into them from the plaza.

Hopi homes, or pueblos, were four- to five-story rectangular apartment-like buildings with flat roofs. The floor of one room was the ceiling of the room below. Homes were constructed out of flat slabs of sandstone (a soft, reddish or yellowish rock) and a kind of mud called "adobe."

Villagers relax on one of the flat roofs of a sandstone pueblo.

People lived in the outer rooms in spring, summer, and fall because there was more sunlight. They cooked, made pottery, wove fabric, and ground corn on the balconies and terraces. During the winter, the Hopi lived in the inner rooms, where they also stored their food.

The Hopi had simple furnishings. In the middle of the inner room in which the Hopi cooked, there was a stone- or clay-lined fire pit. The smoke rose through a hole in the roof. Religious statues could be found in small alcoves—Hopi women built small shrines to the household gods.

A wooden pole hung down from the ceiling to hold clothes. People sat on built-in stone benches. They slept on the floor, wrapped in blankets. By day, the blankets could be rolled up to become extra seats, much like our present-day futons.

The brush, grass, and mud ceilings were supported by heavy wooden beams. Simple tools like digging sticks and hoes for farming and stone tools for grinding corn were stored in the home. There was also a food storage bin. Various baskets and clay pots were always handy for cooking and storing food.

The Hopi didn't believe that people could actually own land. Village councils divided the tribal land so that each family had enough to raise their vegetables. If a man failed to use his land, he could lose it to his village group or to his nephews.

Opposite: Men gathered in the underground **kiva**, *which was in the center of every Hopi community.*
Below: Women made clay pots and decorated them with bold, striking designs.

Family Life

The Hopi had strict rules for picking marriage partners. Girls chose the boys they wanted to marry during group rabbit hunts. Girls took corn cakes to the hunt and traded them for rabbits. By giving leftover cakes to one boy, a girl showed she had chosen him. The boy talked the matter over with his parents. A few days after the hunt, the girl sat outside her house waiting for the boy to visit. If he came, the courtship began. If the girl later took a basket of *piki*, a thin, water bread, to the boy's home, it meant she wanted to marry him. If the boy ate the *piki*, he agreed to the marriage.

Weddings were festive. Men in the groom's family had the job of weaving the bride's white wedding robe with red, black, and green trim. The men wove a second robe for the bride to carry to the ceremony. This robe would cover the bride when she died and went to the spirit world.

The Hopi bride-to-be and her mother made many baskets and filled them with cornmeal. The future bride visited the groom's mother, bringing baskets of corn. The groom received the largest basket, which would be buried with him when he died.

Before the wedding, things got rather messy! The families of the bride and groom had a mud fight in the village square. While they threw mud, the relatives made jokes about each other. This pretend fight helped both families get rid of any bad feelings before the marriage took place.

Most couples wanted to have children. When a child was born, it was washed in warm water and rubbed with ashes from the wood of a juniper tree. The Hopi thought this would keep the baby from becoming hairy. For thirteen days, mother and child stayed home, where a fire burned to keep bad spirits away. Before daybreak on the twentieth day, the child was given his or her name.

The Hopi wove brightly colored ceremonial sashes, such as this one.

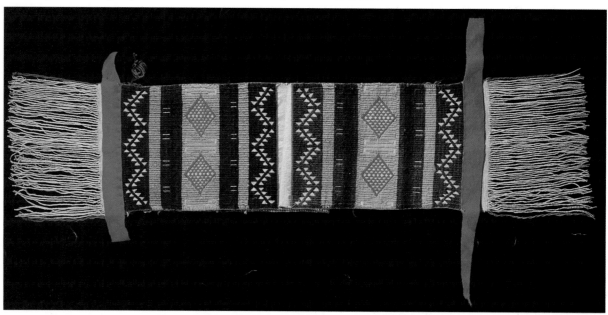

A bride-to-be and her mother weave baskets that they will fill with corn for the groom's family.

Hopi babies spent their first six months on padded, wooden cradle boards. They were strapped to the boards and wrapped in cotton blankets, which made it easy for adults to carry them around. (New babies like the feeling of being wrapped tightly, or swaddled.) As the babies grew older, they played freely in the village with their dolls and toy animals. Parents expected children to learn about nature. They were taught not to injure animals or people, to be kind, and to respect their elders.

Children were hardly ever punished for misbehaving. They knew the rules: If a child did not behave, an evil spirit would take him or her away.

Teenage Hopi boys joined the *kiva* societies and learned the secret ceremonies. Clay figures and rattles for chanting were some of the things kept there. The boys sat in the warm *kivas* during the winter months to hear Hopi elders tell stories about their history and beliefs. The boys learned how to dress for ceremonies as well as how to chant and pray. Spinning and weaving cloth, preparing leather hides, and making tools were taught as well.

Food Gathering and Preparation

Since much of the land was dry, water was an important factor in Hopi agriculture. There were droughts, and after heavy summer rains, there were also floods. Sometimes the solution to a water problem was to plant crops in floodplains, then wait for floods to water them.

Maize, or corn, was the staple food, and the Hopi grew several varieties. They used simple wooden digging sticks to push away dry earth until they got to the wet ground underneath. Then the Hopi planted several kernels of corn in each hole to ensure that one would sprout. Because the Hopi lacked water, they sang and prayed to their corn to encourage it to grow. They farmed their dry land this way for centuries without irrigation.

Piki bread was an important Hopi staple that was usually made with blue cornmeal. Hopi girls were taught the art of making *piki* when they were little. First, the blue cornmeal was mixed in boiling water to make the batter. Then, after lightly greasing a stone griddle with toasted squash seeds, the Hopi women used their fingers to delicately spread a thin layer of batter over the griddle. The bread, which cooked in seconds, was then rolled up. As the rolls cooled, they became crispy. For ceremonies and special occasions, red *piki* was prepared with white cornmeal and water in which the red blossoms of a desert flower had steeped.

A man casts an offering of cornmeal to the spirits before tending his field.

Another Hopi dish called *chukuviki* was served on special occasions, such as weddings. Moistened cornmeal was made into a stiff dough, then shaped into crescents. Each crescent was wrapped and steamed or sometimes dropped in boiling water.

Maize was boiled or roasted on the cob. It was also made into a drink called *pinole*, a mix of ground roasted dry corn and cold water. Beer was also made from maize. In addition to providing food and drink, maize had other uses. Small stalks were used for bedding, and corncobs were used for pipe bowls.

For important ceremonies the Hopi cooked in a deep pit, which they called a *pikami-quopko*. The pit was dug and lined with stones. A fire was then started. When it became red-hot, heating the surrounding stones, the wood was removed. Then food was added, often wrapped in corn husks or plant leaves. The food was cooked by the heated stones.

Sweet bread was one of the foods baked in a pit. It was prepared with

A Hopi woman grinds cornmeal.

cornmeal ground from ears of sweet corn that had been roasted in the husk and then dried.

The Hopi grew other vegetables in addition to maize. Beans and squash were usually planted between the rows of Indian corn. Dried corn and beans were boiled together to make a dish called *succotash*. Squash was prepared by peeling the plant, cutting it in half, and sun-drying it. Squash seeds were roasted and eaten whole.

Women were in charge of gathering and preparing agave, a wild edible plant with many uses: The meat was eaten, and its juice was fermented into a drink. Groups of women selected a roasting place, and the men prepared the pit. It was filled with wood, and a layer of stones was placed over the wood. Once the fire was lit, it continued to burn until there was no more fuel. Cooking the agave took two days. The heart of the plant's crown was the sweetest part, and it was usually saved as candy for Hopi boys and girls.

Many different kinds of cactus were used for food and healing purposes. The Hopi knew just when the prickly pear fruit would ripen and fall, and they made sure to gather it before the wild animals had a chance to eat it.

Mesquite was another rich supply of food. After the small tree ripened in late summer, its pods were gathered and dried in the sun, then pounded into a sweet-tasting flour. This flour was then moistened until it hardened into a cake, which could be stored for a long time.

One of the most popular wild plants was the nut of the piñon pine. The nuts were gathered by shaking the tree and picking up nuts that fell to the ground. Another useful wild plant was the

cattail, which provided not only food but also material for mats, baskets, cradles, and rope. The flowering head of the cattail was used for bread, and the roots were steamed in a pit or roasted over an open fire and then eaten.

Above: This storage jar was made by a Hopi woman more than 200 years ago.
Below: The Hopi were very skilled at applying beautiful geometric designs to pots such as this one.

16

Women use a long pole to knock off the fruit of the giant saguaro cactus. Inset: A woman holds several varieties of maize, a staple of the Hopi diet.

Hunting and Fishing

The Hopi hunted large and small animals. Deer were especially important. Hopi hunters armed with bows and arrows formed a large circle around the deer when the animals were feeding.

While the deer were busy eating, the men sneaked up on their prey. Some of the men walked quietly into the center of the circle and slowly forced the deer toward the hunters.

Another common hunting technique involved setting fire to the grass around

A group of men hunt rabbits, which they have herded into a net.

the deer herd. The frightened deer huddled in the center of the circle and were easily caught.

Other big game hunted were antelope, mountain sheep, and buffalo. Small game were also hunted. Rabbits were the main source of fresh meat, and catching them became a community affair. Groups of Hopi hunters drove the rabbits into nets and used throwing sticks to kill the rabbits. The sticks bounced, and sometimes a hunter hit more than one rabbit with one throw.

When the Hopi men hunted rabbits for everyday use, women would accompany them. When Hopi men hunted rabbit to use in their ceremonies, however, women did not go with them. The group of hunters always included the medicine man, who made offerings to the spirits of the rabbits. Even today, the Hopi politely tell the rabbits that they were put on Earth to provide food for the Hopi people, and they ask the animals' forgiveness before killing them.

The bow and arrow were most commonly used for hunting. The bows were made from saplings (young trees) and were around 3 inches thick. Arrow shafts were created from tree shoots. The feathers that were attached to the shaft came from the wings or tails of turkeys or crows. Arrows were carried, points down, in a quiver made of buckskin or rawhide.

Hopi men fished with scoops made of willow. The scoops were too heavy for young boys. Instead, boys used long fishing poles and attached cotton lines to them. The hooks were made from the curved spines of the barrel cactus.

Fish were usually eaten fresh and not dried. Cooking the fish by broiling it or boiling it with finely ground corn was primarily a man's job.

Political and Social Organization

The Hopi belonged to groups called clans. Members of a clan thought of themselves as relatives of a large family, even though they were not all related to one another. The clans, which sometimes had hundreds of members, were named after birds, mammals, reptiles, insects, or sometimes foods, such as corn or squash. The clans were one of the most important features of Hopi social organization. The children in a family belonged to their mother's clan.

The Hopi lived in eleven villages on or near the First and Second Mesas. (There were only six residential sites on the Third Mesa.) The binding relationships of the different communities with one another represented Hopi social management.

There was no central tribal leadership. Each Hopi village governed itself. Their leaders were the village chief, who was called the *kikmongwi*, and his advisors. The chief's role was inherited.

The traditional Hopi household—family members directly related to the female head of household—consisted of maternal relatives who lived in rooms and houses next to one another. A man joined his wife in her home and helped his in-laws by working in the fields and constructing and repairing houses that belonged to his wife's relatives. Married men lived with their wives, but they regarded the households of their mothers and sisters as their real homes. Hopi men often returned to the homes of their birth to participate in ceremonies and to exercise authority over younger family members.

One Hopi household in each of a village's clans was the custodian of the clan's religious ceremonies. The oldest woman of the household was the head of the clan, but the "real" clan leader was her brother, or maybe a maternal uncle. This man would perform the rituals for the benefit of all clan members.

Clothing

Before explorers from Europe arrived in the Southwest, many Hopi wore clothing made from animal skins or cotton woven on a loom. On their feet, they wore sandals made of woven plant fibers or moccasins sewn from animal skins. Some type of jewelry was also worn. The people wore distinctive hairstyles. Young unmarried Hopi girls put their hair up in imitation of squash blossoms or butterfly wings.

Men wore loose-fitting white cotton trousers and shirts with neck holes. Women wrapped themselves in blankets called *mantas*.

Left: Hopi girls often styled their hair in the shapes of two squash blossoms.
Above: In summer, men wore loincloths.

Robes made from rabbit skins helped to keep the Hopi warm in winter. Skilled weavers cut the rabbit skins into thin strips and wove them together with plant fibers to make a strong cloth. People who did not have fur robes wore blankets made from feathers over their cotton clothing.

In the hot summers, men wore a simple cotton loincloth with a cloth sash tied around the waist. Women wore a rectangular piece of cotton cloth that covered the right shoulder and fastened under the left arm. The left shoulder was bare. Women wrapped a woven belt or sash around the waist many times to hold the dress in place. Hopi children ten years old and younger usually wore no clothing during the hot summers.

Games

Hopi children enjoyed many activities. They liked to chase butterflies and birds. They also had special toys and games. Tops were favorites and were made by the men of the tribe. The girls' tops were plain; the boys' tops were painted with red, white, or black bands. Hopi children could play with tops only at certain times. The humming noise they made sounded like the wind, and the Hopi believed tops had the power to bring windy weather. After early spring, tops were put away because wind storms could destroy the newly growing plants.

Another noisy toy was the whizzing stick, also known as the bull-roarer. It was a thin piece of wood with a long cord attached to one end. When the wood was whirled quickly around the head, it made a loud roar.

The whirligig was a similar toy. It was made of a flat piece of pottery or stone with one or more cords attached on either side. When the cords were pulled, the disks whirled around.

Hopi boys and girls loved to play games. Older boys enjoyed the witch game. The player picked to be the witch was given a small drum. He then had to hide and let the others find him. If they headed off in the wrong direction, the "witch" would beat upon his drum, and then quickly run to another secret spot.

The most popular sport among boys was kickball racing, which was a relay game. Teams of barefoot runners kicked a ball in front of them for 20 miles. It was usually played in spring and early summer because the Hopi believed that kickball racing made the streams run.

Pastimes for girls and women included games of skill. They enjoyed trying to juggle four stones at once or toss necklaces over a corncob standing on its end.

Young Hopi men play the popular sport of kickball racing.

Religious Life

The Hopi believed that they came from the underworld through a place known as *sipapu*, and that when they died, they would return to their place of origin. *Sipapu* was thought to be located at the bottom of the Little Colorado River Canyon, just above the place where it joins the Colorado River.

There are many Hopi legends that have been told for generations. These tales are a part of the rich Hopi mythology. One legend that relates to the origin of the Hopi people is told at every family's fireside.

A long time ago, the Hopi lived in the underworld beneath the surface of the Earth. They raised corn and other foods and celebrated their traditional ceremonies. There came a time when the rains stopped and the crops failed. Looking up toward the clouds, they could see what appeared to be a hole in the sky. They thought there might be another country on that side. Maybe, they thought, it rains there, and the crops grow more abundantly.

The chief talked it over with the elders, or wise old men. They decided to find out what was on the other side of the sky. The chief called a hawk. He instructed the hawk to fly up toward the sky and return with a report of what he had found.

The hawk flew, circled around and around, and finally returned, exhausted. He told the people he wasn't able to fly high enough because his wings gave out.

The chief and the elders decided to try again. This time, however, they sent for the mockingbird. They gave the mockingbird the same instructions.

He flew up higher and higher and disappeared. After a long time, he returned, but all he reported was that he was not able to see what was on the other side of the sky.

There was much discussion among the chief and elders. This time, they sent for the bluebird. The bluebird started to fly. A long time passed, and he finally returned. Yes, he told the people, there was a country up there beyond the sky—a land that would make good fields, and where there are springs and rain clouds.

The chief told his people to prepare food for their journey. Then he sent for the medicine man and asked him to make a ladder which they could climb. The medicine man planted a reed, which grew quickly and sturdily. In a little while, it reached the hole in the sky and kept on growing. The people knew it had grown through the hole and reached the country on the other side.

They started climbing up the reed, the chief in the lead. When they had all reached the other side, they saw that everything was just as the bluebird had described. The chief then told the people where they could build homes and what land they could cultivate.

After the Hopi had planted their crops and built houses, the chief's young daughter died. The chief felt badly because he did not know what would become of her spirit. When he looked down the hole through which they had climbed from the underworld, he saw his daughter happily playing with other children. The chief knew then that the underworld is where everyone went after living in this world.

The Hopi believed that an important group of spirits called *kachinas* brought rain and general well-being. Some were said to live in the mountains and waters, and others lived in the clouds and the underworld.

According to Hopi tradition, *kachinas* came to Hopi villages long ago. When the Hopi needed help, the *kachina* danced, causing rain to fall so that crops would grow. The *kachinas* gave gifts and taught the Hopi people hunting and crafts.

Then one day the *kachinas* and the Hopi got into a dispute and the *kachinas* left. They refused to return, but they did agree that the Hopi people could wear ceremonial masks and impersonate, or pretend to be, *kachinas*.

Kachina masked dances were performed from January to June each year. Hopi children received dolls representing various *kachinas*. These dolls were used only to teach the children about the *kachinas'* virtues; the dolls were not supposed to be played with.

Children were given kachina *dolls for religious inspiration rather than for play.*

In February, the Hopi impersonated *kachinas* in a Bean Dance. The *"kachinas"* brought samples of new bean sprouts. The chief *"kachina"* was the main performer. He wore white, except for his red moccasins and a bit of blue over one shoulder. In one hand, he carried a small wand; in the other hand, he held a gourd containing sacred water. The chief's lieutenant appeared in the dance, dressed in a high, cone-shaped mask that was painted with many colors.

Before returning to their spiritual homes each year, the *kachinas* visited the Hopi for one last time during a ceremony in July. They danced at night, and then they disappeared.

According to Hopi legend, a bluebird helped the people find their way out of the underworld.

The Spanish explorer Francisco de Coronado talks with members of a Pueblo tribe.

European Contact

The Hopi had their land to themselves until A.D. 1540, when the Spanish explorer Francisco de Coronado and his soldiers arrived in the Southwest from Mexico, seeking "cities paved with gold." Instead, Coronado found pueblos filled with poor, hard-working people. He remained there just the same. Coronado's men were the first Europeans to reach the Grand Canyon in northern Arizona and to travel up the Rio Grande valley.

Eventually, the Spanish left the area to pursue other lands, but they returned in 1598. The explorer Juan de Oñate led an expedition into New Mexico and brought along cattle and other domestic animals.

The arrival of the Spanish created problems for the Hopi. The Spanish forced the natives to pay taxes. Sometimes the Spanish forced the Hopi to become their slaves. The Hopi and other Native Americans eventually benefited, however, from the new animals brought by the Spanish— horses and donkeys for transportation, sheep for wool, and cattle for meat. They learned about new tools made of iron, and about new foods, such as wheat, green peppers, and peaches.

In 1629, the Spanish began to build Christian missions. The Hopi and other Native Americans destroyed them in the Pueblo Revolt in 1680. Led by Popé, a member of the Tewa tribe, the revolt was planned in secret. Popé handed out knotted cards to each village chief and told them to untie one knot each day. When the last knot was untied, on August 10, the revolt began. Within a few days, one quarter of all Spaniards in New Mexico were killed, and most of the churches were burned.

In 1692, a Spanish army under the command of Don Diego de Vargas entered the Southwest. Some of the Pueblo Indians thought de Vargas was sympathetic to them and did not object to Spanish rule. Others, including most Hopi, opposed it.

One Pueblo community after another was able to combine its familiar religion with the practices of Christianity. The Hopi returned to their old pre-Christian way of life. The Spanish were busy settling new cities like Santa Fe and Albuquerque in New Mexico.

In 1821, Spain granted independence to Mexico, and the Hopi territory became a Mexican province. In 1848, however, after Mexico lost a war with the United States, present-day New Mexico and Arizona became part of the United States.

The Hopi Today

As of 1991, there were 9,395 Hopi. The population has grown from about 2,200 in 1900. An increasing number live off the reservations.

There are many issues of concern to the Hopi people today. The economic development of the Hopi's isolated reservation is critical as federal employment opportunities have decreased. Another concern is what the Hopi regard as the theft and improper display of ceremonial objects, such as *kachina* masks and dolls, in museums.

A key issue for the Hopi people in the twentieth century has been land. In 1882, President Chester A. Arthur

Building a house is a community effort.

set aside 2.5 million acres as a Hopi reservation. In the early 1900s, the Hopi protested the intrusion of the Navajo onto their 2.5 million acres of land. In 1936, when the U.S. government divided the land, the Hopi were given exclusive use of close to 500,000 acres. The remaining acreage was called Joint Use Land, to be shared with the Navajo. In 1970, the Hopi sued the Navajo in federal court with the hope of forcing them to leave the Joint Use Land. Various lawsuits and appeals are still pending.

In the 1980s, there was increasing interest by the Hopi's tribal council in solving the Hopi's land dispute with the Navajos. The council also concerned itself with a whole series of internal problems such as alcoholism, drug abuse, suicide, and child abuse. Four Hopi mental health conferences that were held between 1981 and 1984 sought to relate Hopi prophecy to contemporary problems. In a document published in 1987, the tribal council said: "The Hopi way is a living tradition that shapes every aspect of the lives of the Hopi people." It included among its goals the preservation of the Hopi way of life and the protection of sacred places.

Chronology

400–500	The Hopi's ancestors, the Anasazi, begin to settle in multifamily houses.
1200s	A group of Pueblo Indians move south into present-day Arizona and become Hopi.
1300–1540	The Hopi build new mesa towns and develop their way of life.
1540	Francisco de Coronado and his soldiers reach the Southwest; Don Pedro de Tovar and his soldiers arrive at the Hopi village of Oraibi.
1629	The Spanish try to convert the Hopi to Catholicism by forcing them to build Catholic churches.
1680	The Hopi join other Pueblo groups to fight against the Spanish in the historic Pueblo Revolt.
1848	After the Mexican War, New Mexico and Arizona become part of the United States.
1865	U.S. government establishes a policy of sending Native American children to boarding schools to learn white culture and language.
1882	President Chester A. Arthur sets aside 2.5 million acres as a Hopi reservation.
1891	Government surveyors divide Hopi land into smaller plots (allotments).
1934	Congress passes the Indian Reorganization Act, which allows the Hopi to govern themselves through elected tribal councils.
1936	U.S. government reduces the size of Hopi land to almost 500,000 acres, naming the rest Joint Use Land for Hopi and Navajo.
1970	The Hopi sue in federal court to have Navajo removed from Joint Use Land. Legal battles continue into the 1990s.

INDEX

Acknowledgments and Photo Credits
Cover and all artwork by Richard Smolinski.
Pages 10 and 15: ©Peabody Museum - Harvard University, by Hillel Burger; p. 14: Library of Congress; p. 30: Courtesy of the Arizona Historical Society/Tucson (AHS #43439).
Map by Blackbirch Graphics, Inc.